W9-COI-229

E $14.95
Sc   Scarry, Richard
           Richard Scarry's
           best read-it-
           yourself book ever

DATE DUE

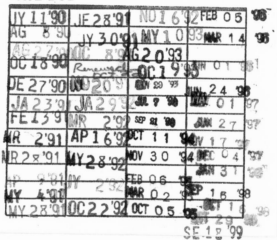

JY 11'90	JF 28'91	NO 16'92	FEB 05 '96	
AG 8'90	JY 30'91	MY 10'93	MAR 14 '96	
AG 27'90	OC 8'91	AG 20'93		
OC 18'90	Renewed OCT 8	OC 19'93	JN 01'96	
DE 27'90	NO 20'91	JUN 29'93	JUN 24 '96	
JA 23'91	JA 29'92	JUL 7'94	MAY 01 '97	
FE 13'91	MR 2'92	SEP 21'94	JUN 27 '97	
MR 2'91	AP 16'92	OCT 11'94	NOV 17 '97	
MR 28'91	MY 28'92	NOV 30'94	DEC 04 '97	JAN 31 '98
AP 2'91	JY 2'92	FEB 06 '95	SEP 16'98	
MY 4'91		MAR 02 '95		
MY 28'91	OC 22'92	OCT 05 '95		

SE 18 '99

AP 18 '00
JY 19 '00
SE 05 00
FE 02 02
JE 17 '08
JY 10 '08

EAU CLAIRE DISTRICT LIBRARY

DEMCO

Richard Scarry's
Best Read-It-Yourself Book Ever

A Collection of 12 Easy-to-Read Stories

Richard Scarry's
Best Read-It-Yourself
Book Ever

A Collection of 12 Easy-to-Read Stories

EAU CLAIRE DISTRICT LIBRARY

A GOLDEN BOOK • NEW YORK
Western Publishing Company, Inc., Racine, Wisconsin 53404

©1990, 1988 Richard Scarry. All rights reserved. Printed in the U.S.A. No part of this book may be reproduced or copied in any form without written permission from the publisher. All trademarks are the property of Western Publishing Company, Inc. Library of Congress Catalog Card Number: 89-51809 ISBN: 0-307-16551-5/ISBN: 0-307-66551-8 (lib. bdg.)   A B C D E F G H I J K L M

77854

TABLE OF CONTENTS

Foreword

"Mom! Dad! Listen to me! I can read!" It's one of the most triumphant moments for any child—and any parent.

Now, of course, your new little reader wants to practice all the time. When children start reading, it takes time for their reading vocabulary to match their spoken vocabulary. They need books with easily recognizable words to encourage their sense of achievement. They need simple sentences, because they can't yet keep track of complicated thoughts on paper—even though they may speak and understand long, complex sentences. And finally, children also need some words they don't know already, to challenge them to further efforts. Stories with these elements draw children into reading independently.

Richard Scarry's Best Read-It-Yourself Book Ever provides all these things. The vocabulary is carefully chosen and monitored to blend familiarity with challenge. Simple sentences, with a few complex ones mixed in, make reading easy and interesting for all children, whether they are getting ready to read, are beginning to read, or are already reading on their own.

Yet reading involves more than just words and sentences, and *Richard Scarry's Best Read-It-Yourself Book Ever* is far more than that. Richard Scarry's humorous characters, situations, and art come to life for children. They'll pick up this book over and over again to follow Smokey the Fireman's adventures with Katie Kitty. They'll enjoy Sniff the Detective's mystery-solving abilities and laugh with Harry and Larry the Fishermen as they struggle to get dinner. Mr. and Mrs. Dr. Doctor juggle their parenting and their careers, as so many real parents must. Children will wonder just what Frances Fix-It is going to repair next, and they'll love Farmer Patrick Pig's predicaments.

Lively, interesting characters and situations combined with ease of reading and a bit of challenge are irresistible to young readers. Your child will return to these stories until every word had been mastered—and after that, too, for the pleasure and comfort of familiar old friends. In the end, that's what *Richard Scarry's Best Read-It-Yourself Book Ever* will become: a beloved old friend.

—Sally R. Bell
Reading Consultant

Smokey,
the Best Fire Fighter Ever

Smokey was a fire fighter.
He loved to put out fires.
One day Smokey had
nothing to do.
So he went to sleep.

Down the street a voice cried,
"Help! Help! My house is
full of smoke!"
It was Katie Kitty.

The fire bell began to ring!
Wake up, Smokey!

Smokey jumped up.

He put on his hat.

He put on his boots.

He put on his raincoat.

He slid down the pole.

He jumped into his fire engine.

Clang! Clang! went the bell.
Officer Bob stopped the cars.
Hurry, Smokey!

EAU CLAIRE DISTRICT LIBRARY

Oh, no! A pie truck was
in the way.
Pies went flying.
The pieman went flying, too.

They all landed in
Smokey's fire engine!
But Smokey kept on going.
Katie Kitty needed his help.

Smokey hurried up the ladder.
He saved Katie Kitty.
"Oh, thank you, Smokey!"
said Katie.

18

Then Smokey turned his hose
on the fire.
SWOOOSH!
The fire was out.

Smokey turned his hose
on his fire engine.
SWOOOSH!
His fire engine was red again.

Smokey turned his hose
on the pieman.
SWOOSH!
The pieman was clean again.

Then everyone went inside.
They wanted to see what
the fire was all about.
Oh, my! A pie was in the oven.
It had burned up.
What a mess!

So they cleaned up the mess.
Then Katie Kitty made
another pie.
And everyone sat down
and ate it.

Farmer Pig's Busy Day

Patrick Pig was a farmer.

His wife was a farmer, too.

Her name was Penny.

They got up early every morning.

"Here is your breakfast,"
Penny said.
"It is a pickle."
"Good! I love pickles,"
said Patrick.

Farmer Pig put on his straw hat.
Then he went outside. He had
to feed the hens and chicks.
He put the eggs in a basket.

He went to the barn.
He milked the cow.
Oh, no! The cow
knocked over the milk.
What a mess!

Next Patrick got
into his truck.
He went to meet the train.
A box was coming
by train.

In the box was a new hat
for Penny.
Patrick tried it on for fun.
"Look at you!"
said the train man.

29

When Patrick got home,
he gave the hat to Penny.
"Thank you, my dear," she said.
She gave Patrick a big hug.
Then she gave him a pickle
for lunch.

30

After lunch Patrick brought
the hay in from the fields.
His cow loved to eat
hay and straw.

Patrick put the hay into the barn.
Oh, no! The wind blew his hat off.

The hat flew up into the barn.
Patrick wanted to get it back.

But first he needed a drink.
So Patrick went
to the well.
Oops! He fell in!

Penny Pig came along.
"What are you doing
down there?" she said.
Then she pulled him out.
But her new hat fell in!

She pulled that out, too.
She put it back on.
And then she and Patrick
went in for supper.
They ate seven pickles.

And Farmer Pig's cow found
Farmer Pig's hat in
Farmer Pig's barn.
And Farmer Pig's cow ate
Farmer Pig's hat for supper.

Sniff Catches the Robber

Sniff is a detective.

He helps people find things.

He helps catch bad people.

He thinks with his head.

And he smells with his nose.

One day Sniff got a phone call.
It was Chief Hound.
"We need your help," Hound said.
"Meet me at Mrs. Jewel's house."
"I will be there right away,"
said Sniff.

"How can I help?" Sniff asked.
Hound said, "This is Mrs. Jewel.
And this is her bracelet box.
Mrs. Jewel likes to wear
a lot of bracelets.
She likes it even better than
eating pumpkins. She grows
pumpkins in her garden.

"Every morning Mrs. Jewel opens
her bracelet box. She takes
out some bracelets to wear.
Every morning she sees
that another bracelet is missing."

41

"I have lost seven bracelets,"
said Mrs. Jewel.
"This must stop!
Soon I will have no bracelets left."

"Have you gone out this week?"
asked Sniff.
"Yes," said Mrs. Jewel, "but only
to water my pumpkins."

"Has anyone been here?"
asked Sniff.
"No," said Mrs. Jewel.
"Have you left a window open?"
"No," said Mrs. Jewel, "and I always
lock the back door."

Sniff thought and thought.
At last he said,
"I will help you.
I will stay here.
I will be quiet.
I will watch. I will listen."

The sun went down.
Mrs. Jewel went to sleep.
She made lots of noise.
She snored and snored.

Sniff listened.

He heard something.

He thought he smelled a rat.

Raffles Rat was in the room!

Raffles quickly went to
Mrs. Jewel's bracelet box.
He opened it.
He took out a bracelet.
Raffles climbed up the chimney.
Sniff could not catch him.

Raffles Rat had escaped
up the chimney.
"If he comes back again,
I know how to catch him,"
said Sniff to himself.
"I have just the right kind
of bracelet for him."

The next night Sniff watched again.
But he soon fell asleep.
Raffles Rat came down the chimney.
He saw a small bracelet
that opened and closed.
It was the right size for his wrist.
He snapped it shut on his wrist.

Raffles Rat then climbed quickly
up the chimney.
Oh, look! Sniff has been dragged
out of his chair.
Sniff had tied the small bracelet
to his leg with a string.
The bracelet was a handcuff!
Raffles could not get the bracelet
off his wrist and escape.

51

Mrs. Jewel pulled Raffles
out of the chimney.
Chief Hound came into the room.
"Where did you hide
the bracelets, Raffles?"
asked Chief Hound.
Raffles told him.

Chief Hound found eight bracelets
in a pumpkin in the garden.
"We must celebrate," said Mrs. Jewel.
So they all sat down and had
pumpkin pie.
Then Chief Hound took Raffles
off to jail.
Raffles will never steal
another bracelet again,
especially not one with
a string on it!

Frances Fix-It's
Busy Day

Frances Fix-It is always busy.
People are always calling her.
They say, "Please, Frances,
fix this for me."
Then Frances goes to fix it.

Mr. Goat's water pipes were leaking.
He called Frances.
She went and fixed them.
She got a little wet.

A boat hit a rock.
It made a hole in the side
of the boat.

Frances fixed the hole.
She can fix just about anything.

A tire fell off the fire engine.
Frances put it back.

Mrs. Cat's car would not go.
The engine would not start.
Frances turned the car over.
Frances hit the engine
with her hammer.
The engine started.

59

The policeman called Frances.
His motorcycle would not go.
"You have no gas," said Frances.
She put gas in the motorcycle.
Then the policeman
went after a car.
It was going too fast.

A streetlight would not work.
Frances fixed it.
Look out, Frances!

There was shouting on the train.
The engine had jumped off the track.
No one who tried could get it
back onto the track.
But Frances could.

Frances stopped at the Pig family's house.
She had to fix their television set.

Mother Pig ran into the room.

"Help! Help!" she cried.

"My oven is doing something funny.

I think it is going to blow up!"

Frances ran into the kitchen.
The oven BLEW UP!
Mother had been making fudge.
Now it was all over the kitchen.

Frances had no time to fix up
THAT mess!

It was time to go home.
But Frances' truck had a flat tire.
And Frances had fudge on her hands.

She had to call a tow truck.
When she got home, she took a bath.

69

Freddie Fox
Visits Dr. Doctor

Freddie Fox is in the doctor's office.
His mother is with him.
They are waiting for the doctor.

Other people are waiting, too.
The doctor is late.

The telephone rings.
Dr. Doctor's nurse answers it.
She says, "Which Dr. Doctor
do you want to see?

Mr. Dr. Doctor helps mothers
when they have babies.
Mrs. Dr. Doctor helps children
stay well."

The doctor is coming.
No. Two doctors are coming!

"Good morning," says Mr. Dr. Doctor.
"Good morning," says Mrs. Dr. Doctor.
"Good morning," say all the people
who are waiting.

75

Freddie and his mother get up.
They follow Mrs. Dr. Doctor.

"How do you feel, Freddie?"
asks Mrs. Dr. Doctor.
"I feel fine," says Freddie.
"Well, let me see," says the doctor.

"Open wide!" the doctor tells Freddie.
She looks in his mouth.
She looks in his ears.
She looks all over him.

"Freddie, you look just fine!"
says the doctor.
"My, you are also getting
big and strong.
Now, do not get sick.
Then I will not have
to see you for a while.

"Now I have a surprise for
both of you.
I am going to have a baby,"
the doctor says.

"Oh, boy!" says Freddie.

"Will it be a girl or a boy?"

"We do not care," says Mrs. Dr. Doctor.

"Just as long as it is well, like you."

"Will Mr. Dr. Doctor help
when you have the baby?" asks Freddie.
"He will be there if he can,"
says Mrs. Dr. Doctor.
"But only just like any other father.

"Our friend Dr. Bandage will help,"
says Mrs. Dr. Doctor.
"He is a good doctor.
He helps a lot of mothers
when they have babies."

"May I play with the baby?"
asks Freddie.
"When the baby gets old enough,"
says Mrs. Dr. Doctor.
"Then he, or she, may
play with you."

Isn't that nice?

The Best Fish Ever

Mother Cat has nine kittens.
They live in a big house
near the sea.
Mmmmm! What is that
yummy smell?

87

That smell is fish.
The house always
smells of fish.
The cats love fish.
They eat fish more than
anything else.

Mother Cat has two brothers.
One is Uncle Harry.
The other is Uncle Larry.
Every morning they go
to the dock.
They get into their boat.

Every morning the nine kittens
go to the dock.
They wave good-bye to
Uncle Harry and Uncle Larry.

Then the two uncles
begin to row.
They row out to sea.
They try to catch a fish
for dinner.

One morning the sea was rough.
Uncle Harry caught a soup can.
Uncle Larry did not catch anything.

Uncle Harry caught a boot.
Uncle Larry did not catch anything.

Uncle Harry caught an old tire.
Uncle Larry did not catch anything.
What will the family eat
if they don't catch a fish?

Look! Uncle Larry
caught a fish.
What a fish!

He paddled back to shore.
Mother Cat and the nine kittens
were waiting on the dock.
They were all very happy.

That night the Cat family had
the best fish dinner ever.

Smokey's Day Off From Work

It was Smokey's day off from work.
"I need some rest,"
he said to Katie Kitty.
"How about spending a quiet day
in the country with me?"
"That sounds very nice," said Katie.

So Smokey and Katie
went on a picnic.
Smokey brought sandwiches.
He brought milk.
Katie brought some blueberry pies.
What a good lunch they had!

Then they went to the pond.
They watched the frogs swimming.
It was very quiet.
Smokey almost fell asleep.

All at once they heard loud voices.
The voices said, "Help! Help!
Come quick!"

Smokey and Katie saw
Patrick and Penny Pig.
"Our barn is on fire!"
shouted Penny.
"We are here!" said Smokey.
"We will help!

"Are all your animals safe?"
asked Smokey.

"Yes," said Patrick.

Smokey had to think fast.

He did not have his fire engine.

He did not have his fire hose.

What could he do?

105

"Quick!" shouted Smokey.
"We must go to the well!"
At the well they met Farmer Fox.
He wanted to help, too.

Smokey told them all what to do.
Patrick got water in pails from the well.
He gave them to Penny.

Penny gave them to Katie.
Katie gave them to Smokey.
Smokey was up on a ladder.

109

Smokey threw water on the fire.
Farmer Fox was waiting.

Smokey threw down the empty pails to him.

111

Farmer Fox ran with the
empty pails to the well.
He gave the pails to Patrick.
Then Patrick filled them again.

Soon the fire was out.
"Thank you, Smokey!"
said Patrick and Penny.
"You saved our barn."

"Our day was not quiet,"
said Smokey. "But we all did
what I do best when I work.
We put the fire out!
Now we can rest—"
"And have some more pie!"
said Katie.
And they all ate lots of pie.

Farmer Pig's Helper

One morning Patrick Pig
ate breakfast.
"We need someone to help us
on our farm," he said.

Patrick got into his truck.
He drove to town.

He saw someone.

"What is your name?" asked Patrick.

"Thumble," answered the man.

"Would you help us
on our farm?" asked Patrick.

"I would love to,"
said Thumble.

"First you must learn to
drive our truck," said Patrick.
"Drive us back to the farm."

They had to cross a bridge.

"This is not the way
to drive our truck,"
said Patrick.

120

Luckily Farmer Fox came by.
He pulled them out
of the water.

121

Thumble drove to the farm.
He went through the gate.
He did not open it first.

Thumble drove through the yard.
He drove through Penny's wash.

"Would you milk our cow?"
asked Patrick.
"I would love to," said Thumble.

124

Thumble milked the cow.
But then he spilled the milk.

"Would you water our
pickle garden?" asked Patrick.

"I would love to," said Thumble.
Thumble tried to water the garden.
He watered Penny's kitchen instead.

127

They sat down and had supper.
"Would you clear the table?"
asked Penny.
"I would love to," said Thumble.

Thumble cleared the table.
"You are of no help to us,"
said Patrick.
"We need a helper who can help.
I will drive you back to town."

Patrick drove the truck.
They had to cross a bridge.
Oh, dear!
Patrick really does need
someone who can help!

Sniff's Best Case Ever

One day Sniff woke up.

It was raining.

"I am tired," he thought.

"I am glad I have
nothing to do."

Just then Sniff got a phone call.

It was the police chief
in another city.

"We need your help!" he said.

"I will come right away,"
said Sniff.

Sniff was not happy.

He did not want to go.

The next day was his birthday.

He wanted to stay home.

He wanted to eat cake and ice cream.

132 But Sniff had work to do!

Sniff had to take the train.
He had to ride all night.
Hurry, Sniff!
Don't miss the train!

133

"Look at all these
scary guys!" Sniff thought.
"Who are they?

"They are wearing sunglasses.
They are looking at me!"

Sniff went to his bedroom
on the train.
He hid under the bed.

More scary guys got on the train.
They all carried violins.
Sniff was afraid.
What were they up to?

137

At last it was morning.
Sniff came out from
under the bed.
He saw all the scary guys.
They were looking at him.

The sun was shining.
So Sniff put on sunglasses, too.
He stepped outside.

But the scary guys threw away
their sunglasses.
Then Sniff saw who they were.
They were all police chiefs.
They had come from many cities.

They were playing violins.
They were singing,
"Happy birthday to you,
dear Sniffy."
It was a surprise party!

So they all went to the beach.
They played ball.
They went for a swim.
They ate cake and ice cream
until they could eat no more.

And Sniff had the best
birthday ever!

144

Frances Builds
a Crazy Thing

One day Frances said to herself,
"I am always fixing things.
Why don't I make something new
that does not need to be fixed?"
She went to the closet.
She took out many things.

Frances worked for days
in her workshop.
People could hear her.
But they could not see her.

"Maybe she is fixing a boat,"
said Reddy Fox.
"Or a bathtub," said Big Hilda Hippo.

147

Then one day Frances called her friends.
It was time for them to see
what she had been working on.
It looked something like an AIRPLANE!

"But will it fly?" asked Bob Cat.
"I will show you," said Frances. 149

Frances got into her airplane.
"Everyone stand back," she said.
She started the airplane.
The airplane took off from the ground.
The airplane flew!

The airplane flew straight up.
My, it flew fast.
It flew like a bird.

Then Frances flew the airplane
upside down.
Do not fall out, Frances!
I hope you are wearing your seat belt.
And do not bump into that other airplane.

Frances flew through
Farmer Patrick Pig's barnyard.

Be careful, Frances!
You do not want to hurt yourself!
Or the chickens!

Frances flew past Farmer Fox's tractor.

Look out, Frances!

Duck down, Farmer Fox!

The airplane flew through the cornfield.
It scared the crows.

Finally the airplane flew straight down.

It crashed!

Well, now, Frances. Here is something new
that DOES need to be fixed.

And I know that you can fix it.

And you know it, too.

Don't you?

A Hospital Story

One day Mr. Dr. Doctor
was at the hospital.
He had just helped Mrs. Bunny.
Mrs. Bunny had five new babies.
Then Mr. Dr. Doctor got a call.
It was Mrs. Dr. Doctor.
"Our baby is coming," she said.
"Stay at the hospital.
My sister Sally will take me there."

Mr. Dr. Doctor was very happy.
Then he got another call.
"My mother needs you,"
said a little girl.
Her name was Molly.
Now, Mr. Dr. Doctor wanted
to be with Mrs. Dr. Doctor.
But he had to help Molly's mother first.

So Mr. Dr. Doctor got into an ambulance.
He was on his way to Molly's house.

Meanwhile, Mrs. Dr. Doctor
got into Sally's car.
They were on their way
to the hospital.

Mr. Dr. Doctor saw Sally's car.
He called to Mrs. Dr. Doctor,
"I hope it is a boy."
But Mrs. Dr. Doctor was hoping
for a girl.

Mr. Dr. Doctor got to Molly's house.

He ran in the front door.

He tripped.

"Where is your mother?" he asked.

"In the bedroom," said Molly.

Mr. Dr. Doctor was just in time.
Molly's mother had a baby.

Mr. Dr. Doctor took everyone
to the hospital.
They would rest there.

Mr. Dr. Doctor went to
Mrs. Dr. Doctor's room.
He tripped.
Dr. Bandage was there.

Look! Mrs. Dr. Doctor has a new baby.
No! She has *two* new babies—
a boy *and* a girl!
Mr. and Mrs. Dr. Doctor are very happy.

171

It is a few months later.
Mr. and Mrs. Dr. Doctor come to work.
They have their babies,
Billy and Bonnie, with them.
I think Billy and Bonnie will grow up
to be good doctors, just like their
mommy and daddy.
Don't you hope so?

The Day That
Nothing Happened

One day Uncle Harry
and Uncle Larry
got into their boat.
They rowed out to sea.
They passed a buoy.
A bird was sitting on it.

They started to fish.
Uncle Harry caught a lobster.
The lobster bit his nose.
"Ouch!" he said.
He threw the lobster back
into the water.

174

Uncle Larry caught a crab.
The crab bit his hand.
"Ouch!" he said.
He threw the crab back
into the water.

A fireboat was on the way
to a fire.
It almost ran into them.
"Look out!" said Uncle Larry.
Uncle Harry rowed out of the way
just in time.

They saw a boat
with a family on it.
A baby fell off the boat.
"Hurry! We must save the baby,"
said Uncle Larry.

178

They saved the baby
from the cold water.
They brought the baby back
to his mother.
"Oh, Thank you! Thank you,"
said the mother.

Then they saw someone standing
on his sinking boat.

They saved him, too.

A helicopter came along.
Someone helped him
into the helicopter.
It took him safely to land.

BUMP!

Was it a whale?
No. It was a submarine.
It had come up from
under the water.

"Get off my submarine,"
said the submarine captain.

"You will have to go back
under the water," said Uncle Harry.
The submarine went back
under the water.
But look! Who is that coming?

It was Speedboat Smiley
in his speedboat.
He bumped into Uncle Harry
and Uncle Larry's boat.
Oh, dear!

Uncle Harry and Uncle Larry
got back into their boat.
They rowed home.

At home Mother Cat asked,
"Did anything exciting happen today?"
"No. Nothing happened,"
said Uncle Larry and Uncle Harry.

Do you think that is right?

Born in 1919, Richard Scarry received his early art training at the Boston Museum of Fine Arts School. During World War II, he served in the army as an art director in the Mediterranean and North Africa. After the war, he moved to New York City to illustrate for several leading magazines and there found his niche illustrating children's books in 1946.

In 1963, Richard Scarry established himself as an author/illustrator with *Adventures of Tinker and Tanker.* His next book, *Richard Scarry's Best Word Book Ever,* became a runaway best-seller. At present, Richard Scarry has over 150 books for children to his credit. His funny animal characters have charmed generations of children into loving books and reading. Richard Scarry now lives in Switzerland with his wife, Patsy, who has also written numerous children's books.

Selected books by Richard Scarry:

EAU CLAIRE DISTRICT LIBRARY

EAU CLAIRE DISTRICT LIBRARY